My Favourite Recipes

First printed 2010
Eaglemoss Publications Group, 1st Floor, Beaumont House,
Kensington Village, Avonmore Road,
London W14 8TS

ISSN 2043-0892
123456789

Reproduction by F E Burmans, UK.
Printed in the EU by Imprimerie Pollina.

My Favourite Recipes
Pasta & Pizza

Front cover: Juliet Piddington/Prima/NMC (t), Marie Louise
Avery/Prima/NMC (bl), Juliet Piddlington/Prima/NMC (br),
8 Martin Brigdale/Prima/NMC, 9 Woman and Home/I Skelton
(t), Jon Whittaker/Prima/NMC (bl), Jon Whittaker/Prima/NMC
(bc), Prima/NMC (br), 10 Tim Winter/Prima/NMC (bl), 11 Susie
M.Eising/StockFood, 12 Juliet Piddington/Prima/NMC, 13 Jon
Whittaker/Prima/NMC, 15-17 David Munns/Prima/NMC,
19 Z.Sandmann/Cimbal/StockFood, 21-23 Jon Whittaker/Prima/
NMC, 25 Juliet Piddington/Prima/NMC, 27 Eric Fenot/
PhotoCuisine, 29 Juliet Piddington/Prima/NMC, 31 EM/Nigel
James, 33 Jon Whittaker/Prima/NMC, 35 Tim Winter/Prima/
NMC, 37 Jean-Blaise Hall/Photocuisine, 39 Jon Whittaker/Prima/
NMC, 41 Tim Winter/Prima/NMC, 43-45 Juliet Piddington/
Prima/NMC, 47-49 Tim Winter/Prima/NMC, 51 Norris/
PhotoCuisine, 53-55 Jon Whittaker/Prima/NMC, 57-59 Iain
Bagwell/Prima/NMC, 61 Marie Louise Avery/Prima/NMC,
63 Juliet Piddington/Prima/NMC, 65 Jon Whittaker/Prima/NMC,
67 Karl Gros/Prima/NMC, 69 Iain Bagwell/Prima/NMC, 71 Susie
M.Eising/StockFood, 73-77 Jon Whittaker/Prima/NMC,
79 Lawton/Photocuisine, 81 Geoff Fenney/Prima/NMC, 83 Juliet
Piddington/Prima/NMC, 85 Jon Whittaker/Prima/NMC, 86 Juliet
Piddington/Prima/NMC, 89 Jon Whittaker/Prima/NMC, 91 Juliet
Piddington/Prima/NMC, 93 David Munns/Prima/NMC.

EM = Eaglemoss Publications Group
NMC = The National Magazine Company

My Favourite Recipes

Pasta & Pizza

My Favourite Recipes

When it comes to speed and variety, it's hard to beat pasta and pizza. Pasta is fast becoming one of our most popular food choices, thanks to its endless versatility. From speedy midweek supper ideas to more elaborate dishes like cannelloni and filled pasta shells, we've got all the recipes you'll need to make the most of this great Italian ingredient.

And you don't always have to reach for the takeaway menu if you fancy a pizza. We've got a great selection of tempting recipes plus timesaving ideas for different bases and easy toppings, so you can whip up a hearty supper in no time. Why not try these fresh Italian flavours and create a new great range of favourite family meals. Enjoy!

Becky Davis

Editor

My Favourite Recipes
Pasta & Pizza

page
26

Quick Parma Ham Pizza

page
30

Macaroni Cheese Pie

My Favourite Recipes

Contents

Prawn & Tomato Pasta

Key to recipe symbols

🕐 *Super Quick*
Ready in under 15 minutes.

🕐 *Quick*
Ready in 30 minutes or less.

🕐 *Make it at the Weekend*
This dish needs a little more attention so make it when you have extra time to spare.

✓ *Easy*
Simple to prepare for most cooks.

✓✓ *Extra Easy*
Simple to prepare, even for an inexperienced cook.

❄ *Freeze it*
This recipe can be frozen.

🌶 *Spicy*
This recipe has a bit of a kick!

N *Contains Nuts*
This recipe contains nuts.

V *Vegetarian*
This recipe is suitable for vegetarians.

The Italian Way

If you're looking for a simple and speedy supper, then think Italian and pick a pizza or pasta. Endlessly versatile, they combine with all kinds of ingredients for a different flavour every time. Here are some handy tips and tasty ideas.

Pizzas are a popular choice with all the family but don't just reach for the takeaway menu. Making your own means you can tailor the toppings to suit your tastes and make it as healthy as you like. Making your base from scratch is simple but takes time (see page 18) so if you want a quick-fix, buy a ready-made one or use a pack of

Spinach, Tomato & Olive Mini Pizzas

Many breads and rolls make great speedy pizza bases.

2 English muffins, halved

2 tablespoons sun-dried tomato paste

½ teaspoon dried mixed herbs

150g (5oz) baby spinach

1 beefsteak tomato, sliced

25g (1oz) pitted black olives, halved

50g (2oz) reduced-fat mozzarella, thinly sliced

● Preheat the grill to high. Lightly toast the muffins. Mix together the tomato paste and herbs. Spread over one side of each muffin half. ● Rinse the baby spinach and place in a pan. Cover and cook for 2 minutes until wilted. Drain well. ● Top the muffins with a slice of tomato, some spinach, olives and mozzarella. Grill for 2–3 minutes until the cheese has melted.

Fast-fix Pizza Ideas

● **READY-MADE PIZZA BASE** Spread a thin base with passata. Top with cooked prawns, capers and a drizzle with garlic oil. Bake until golden. Serve with rocket.

● **NAAN BREADS** Spread garlic and coriander naan breads with Greek yogurt mixed with mango chutney. Top with chunks of ready-made chicken tikka and some fried sliced onions. Drizzle with oil and bake for 10–15 minutes until hot.

● **CRUMPETS** Spread crumpets with pesto sauce and top with caramelised onion relish and a slice of goat's cheese. Grill until golden and starting to melt.

● **BRIOCHE** Top halved brioche rolls with wilted spinach mixed with nutmeg and cream. Finish with sun-dried tomatoes and mozzarella. Grill until hot.

● **CIABATTA** Halve a ciabatta loaf and top with tomato pizza sauce or passata. Scatter over sliced ready-made meatballs or falafel, roasted peppers and grated mild cheese. Bake until golden and heated through.

5 Simple Pasta Sauces

● Heat garlic and herb soft cheese in a pan until melted and smooth. Add lemon juice and black pepper to taste.
● Mix crème fraîche, chopped sun-dried tomatoes and canned salmon.
● Fry sliced garlic and red chilli in olive oil until hot and sizzling. Add chopped anchovies and toss with hot pasta.
● Heat double cream and blue cheese until smooth. Add chopped asparagus.
● Cook fresh sage leaves in melted butter until sizzling. Add your choice of toasted nuts. Serve with filled pasta.

DRIED OR FRESH?

Dried pasta is inexpensive and lasts for ages in the cupboard but if you like filled pasta, buy fresh packs and keep in the freezer. They take just a few minutes to cook from frozen.

Pick Your Pasta

Choose a pasta that matches the type of sauce you are using for best results. Here is a simple guide.
● Thin delicate pastas like spaghetti are best with lighter thin sauces like garlic and chilli or herby butter.
● Thicker shapes like tagliatelle work well with heavier sauces like creamy mushroom or blue cheese.
● Serve pasta with holes or ridges, like penne or conchiglie, with chunky sauces like roasted vegetable or sausage and tomato.
● Small pasta shapes like farfalle and fusilli are good for pasta salads.
● Tiny shapes like mini bow ties or shells are best for soups and broths.

pizza dough or bread mix. You can also use other breads, such as muffins or crumpets instead.

PERFECT PASTA

Pasta is the ultimate speedy ingredient and can be combined with a ready-made sauce, some storecupboard staples or a few leftovers from the fridge for a tasty supper in minutes (see above). As well as fast-fix recipes, pasta can also be turned into cold salads for picnics and packed lunches, warming bakes like lasagne or macaroni cheese and hearty soups like minestrone.

Cookery Secrets… 3 Ways with Pasta

Pasta is incredibly versatile and can be used to create all kinds of different supper dishes.

1 *Pasta salads are ideal for lunches and picnics. Use leftover pasta or cook fresh and rinse under cold water to cool. Try mixing with cooked broccoli, tomatoes, almonds, yogurt and pesto.*

2 *Pasta soups make a delicious and filling meal. Cook onion, aubergine, courgette and tomatoes in stock until tender. Add small pasta shapes and simmer until just tender.*

3 *A pasta bake is a super comforting supper. Mix cooked macaroni with four cheese sauce and halved cherry tomatoes. Top with grated cheese, breadcrumbs and herbs and bake.*

Makeover Magic

*Take a basic recipe, add a few extra ingredients
and you can create a whole new dish. Here are
some clever ways to transform your favourite dishes.*

The classic tomato pasta sauce is easy to make (see opposite page) and endlessly versatile. You can serve it on its own with cooked pasta or add meat, fish or vegetables, use it as a pizza topping or the base for a stew or soup. If you like it spicy, add a pinch of dried chilli flakes or a few drops of Tabasco sauce and if you like it creamy, stir in some double cream or crème fraîche just before serving.

Make it Healthy

● If you are watching the cals, choose a tomato-based pasta sauce rather than a creamy one.
● Use a reduced-fat cheese or pick a strong flavoured cheese like Parmesan so you can use less.
● Add extra vegetables to your pizza toppings and pasta sauces and use less cheese.

NEW LOOK FAVOURITES

You can liven up other favourite pasta dishes too. Add a spoonful of grainy mustard to your macaroni cheese or some chopped sun-dried tomatoes to your Bolognese sauce for a real flavour boost. Look out for different coloured pastas to jazz up plain dishes. Green pasta is coloured with spinach, black with squid ink and orange with carrots or squash.

Mushroom & Pesto Calzone

*For a twist on the classic pizza, try this folded version. Add your
favourite toppings like pepperoni, ham, peppers or tomato sauce.*

290g pack pizza dough mix or
½ x 500g pack bread mix
1 tablespoon olive oil
400g (14oz) mushrooms, sliced
4 tablespoons pesto
125g pack mozzarella, drained and
sliced
1 egg, lightly beaten

● Make up the dough according to the pack instructions. Preheat the oven to

200°C/400°F/Gas 6. ● Heat the oil in a frying pan and cook the mushrooms for 5 minutes until golden. ● Divide the dough in half and roll out each piece to a 25cm (10in) long oval. ● Spread half of each oval with pesto. Top with the mushrooms and mozzarella. ● Brush the edges with egg and fold over. Press the edges to seal and brush with egg.
● Place on an oiled tray and bake for 20–25 minutes until golden and cooked.

PERK UP YOUR PIZZA

There are endless ideas for different pizza toppings but most start with a simple tomato sauce. For a change, spread the pizza base with pesto, cheese sauce, bolognese, barbecue sauce or a soft cheese like ricotta, mascarpone or Quark. Mozzarella is the classic pizza topping but you can use other melting cheeses like Cheddar or red Leicester. For a stronger flavour, dot cubes of blue cheese, like dolcelatte or Gorgonzola, over the top before baking, or scatter the hot pizza with Parmesan shavings made using a potato or vegetable peeler.

Classic Tomato Sauce

This basic recipe is ideal for pasta and pizza toppings. It also freezes well so bake up a large batch for speedy midweek suppers.

Serves 4
Preparation 5 mins
Cooking 20 mins

2 tablespoons oil
1 onion or 3–4 spring onions, chopped
1.1kg (2½lb) tomatoes, peeled, deseeded and diced
2 tablespoons tomato purée
450ml (1pt) vegetable stock
Salt and freshly ground black pepper
1 teaspoon sugar
Handful fresh basil leaves, shredded

2 *Add the vegetable stock to the pan, season with salt, pepper and sugar and cook over a low heat for 15 minutes until thickened.*

1 *Heat the oil in a pan and fry the onion or spring onions over a gentle heat until soft. Add the tomatoes and tomato purée.*

3 *If the sauce is too thick, add a little extra vegetable stock then stir in the shredded basil and check the seasoning before serving.*

VARIATIONS

● **For an extra-rich flavour, add a small glass of red wine to the pan before adding the tomatoes. Bubble until the liquid has reduced then continue.**
● **Add extra vegetables like diced carrots, peppers or fennel with the tomatoes.**
● **If you prefer a smooth sauce, blitz with a hand blender at the end of step 2.**
● **The sauce freezes well so make a large batch when summer tomatoes are at their best and cheapest. Freeze in individual portions. Reheat gently in a pan.**

Serve with...
Serve the sauce with cooked spaghetti, grated Parmesan, basil and crusty bread.

Try Something New

Go beyond the traditional meat and tomato sauces and experiment with new flavours to perk up your pasta and pizzas. Here are some great ideas to try.

With just a couple of tasty additions you can liven up a basic pasta sauce with really delicious results. Try adding capers, red chilli or anchovies to a tomato sauce or just cook gently in olive oil or butter and toss with hot pasta (see below) to pack a real flavour punch. A spoonful of mustard or horseradish really livens up a cheese or creamy sauce, while sweet chilli sauce, pesto or hot peri-peri add depth to a tomato sauce. Try dotting spicy tomato chutney, caramelised onion relish, pickled ginger or peppadew peppers over your pizza for bursts of flavour, or drizzle with chilli oil before serving.

SOMETHING SPECIAL

Inject a touch of luxury to your pasta or pizza with some good quality ingredients – you won't need to use a lot to get an impressive result. Smoked salmon makes a great addition to creamy sauces – if you're going to chop the fish, buy packs of trimmings to save on cost. Wedges of fresh fig are delicious additions to a pizza topping, especially with a few ribbons of Parma ham or

Anchovy & Garlic Pasta

This easy dish is ideal for a speedy and cheap midweek supper.

400g (14oz) long pasta

1 tablespoon olive oil

2 garlic cloves, crushed

50g (2oz) anchovies, drained and roughly chopped

Juice of ½ lemon

2 tablespoons chopped fresh parsley

● Cook the pasta according to the pack instructions until tender. Drain. ● Heat the oil in a pan. Cook the garlic and anchovies over a low heat until soft. ● Add to the pasta with the lemon and parsley. Mix.

Tortellini with Spinach & Cheese Sauce

This tasty dish uses just 4 ingredients and is ready in under half an hour.

2 x 300g packs meat-filled tortellini, such as prosciutto crudo
400g (14oz) baby spinach leaves
350g tub cheese sauce
3 tablespoons chopped fresh parsley
Ciabatta bread, to serve

● Preheat the oven to 190°C/375°F/Gas 5.
● Cook the tortellini in a pan of boiling water according to the pack instructions. Drain and return to the pan. ● Stir in the spinach, cheese sauce and parsley. ● Transfer to an ovenproof dish and bake for 20 minutes until bubbling. Serve with warmed ciabatta.

prosciutto draped in between. For a really luxurious dish, try adding caviar to your pasta. Simply toss cooked pasta with fried shallots and some black lumpfish caviar or add a spoonful or two of pink salmon roe to a salmon or prawn pasta dish for an extra special treat.

SEASONAL SPECIALS

In late spring, make the most of asparagus at its best. Griddle and use as a pizza topping or toss with cooked pasta, lemon zest and some melted butter for a simply delicious supper. In autumn look out for wild mushrooms like ceps or porcini and chanterelles. Fry gently in melted butter and garlic and toss with cooked pasta or scatter over a pizza.

Thai Fish Lasagne

A modern twist on the classic Italian favourite with some zingy flavours.

1 small onion, sliced
1 garlic clove, halved
2 star anise
2.5cm (1in) fresh ginger, roughly chopped
1 stalk lemongrass, chopped
1 red chilli, halved
Zest and juice of 1 lime
400g can coconut milk
4 x 100g (3½oz) fish fillets
8 fresh lasagne sheets
2 heads pak choi, halved and cooked
2 tablespoons chopped fresh coriander

● Place first 8 ingredients in a pan. Add the fish and gently bring to the boil. Cook gently for 3–5 minutes. Drain. ● Cook lasagne according to pack instructions. Drain. ● Layer lasagne, pak choi and fish. Top with a little fish cooking sauce and add coriander and lasagne. ● Finish with more sauce.

Mince & Macaroni Bake

Preparation time 10 minutes ● Cooking time 45 minutes

250g (9oz) minced beef

1 onion, chopped

1 garlic clove, crushed

1 teaspoon dried oregano

Salt and freshly ground black pepper

400g can chopped tomatoes

½ x 500g bag macaroni or other

   short pasta

50g (2oz) butter

50g (2oz) plain flour

600ml (1pt) milk

75g (3oz) mature Cheddar, grated

1 teaspoon smooth mustard, optional

1 Preheat the oven to 180°C/350°F/Gas 4. Dry fry the mince, onion and garlic in a frying pan until the mince is browned all over. Add the oregano and season. Stir in the tomatoes and simmer for 15 minutes. Meanwhile, cook the pasta in a pan of boiling water according to the pack instructions.

2 Melt the butter in a saucepan, then stir in the flour with a wooden spoon. Cook over a medium heat for 2 minutes. Remove from the heat and stir in the milk, a little at a time, until the sauce is smooth. Return to the heat and stir until thickened. Remove from the heat, stir in most of the cheese, the mustard if using and season with salt and black pepper.

3 Drain the pasta and mix with the cheese sauce. Tip the mince mixture into an ovenproof dish, then top with the cheesy pasta. Sprinkle with the remaining cheese. Bake for about 20 minutes until golden and bubbling.

Calories per portion 664 Kcal ● Fat per portion 29g ● Serves 4

Serve with...

Serve this warming bake with garlic bread and a green salad.

Why not try...

While you are cooking, you could make two and pop one in the freezer, covered with cling film or foil. Allow to thaw then bake, covered with foil, for 45 minutes at 200°C/400°F/Gas 6.

🕐 *Quick*   ✓✓ *Extra Easy*

Creamy Smoked Trout Pasta

Preparation time 5 minutes ● Cooking time 15 minutes

500g (18oz) bag short pasta

2 x 130g packs Le Roulé cheese

4 tablespoons crème fraîche or
    double cream

200g (7oz) smoked trout, chopped

Juice of ½ lemon

Freshly ground black pepper

● **1** Cook the pasta in a pan of boiling water according to the packet instructions until tender. Drain and return to the pan. Stir in the cheese and crème fraîche or double cream and stir until melted and smooth.

● **2** Add the smoked trout and a good squeeze of lemon juice and season with freshly ground black pepper. Serve immediately.

Calories per portion 742 Kcal ● Fat per portion 28.2g ● Serves 4

Serve with...

All you need to serve with this quick
and easy dish are some lemon wedges
to squeeze over at the table.

Why not try...

You could use smoked salmon or
peppered mackerel fillets instead
of the trout.

🕐 *Make it at the Weekend* Ⓥ *Vegetarian*

Classic Margherita Pizza

Preparation time 25 minutes plus rising ● Cooking time 30 minutes

500g strong white bread flour

3 teaspoons easy-blend dried yeast

1 teaspoon salt

1 teaspoon sugar

6 tablespoons olive oil

Topping

1 tablespoon olive oil, plus extra

    to drizzle

1 garlic clove, chopped

8 tomatoes, deseeded and diced

½ teaspoon dried thyme

Salt and freshly ground black pepper

25g (1oz) fresh basil, shredded, plus

    whole leaves, to garnish

3 x 125g mozzarella balls, sliced

● **1** Place the flour, yeast, salt and sugar in a bowl and make a well in the centre. Add the oil and about 250ml (9fl oz) warm water and mix to a soft dough. Cover and place in a warm place to rise for about 30 minutes.

● **Step 2** Heat 1 tablespoon oil in a pan and fry the garlic until soft. Add the tomatoes and cook briefly. Stir in the thyme and simmer for 2 minutes. Season to taste with salt and pepper and stir in the basil. Set aside.

● **Step 3** Preheat the oven to 220°C/425°F/Gas 7. Take the dough out of the bowl, knead again on a floured surface and cut into 4 pieces. Knead each piece of dough and roll out to a 20cm (8in) circle.

● **4** Oil 4 18cm (7in) pizza pans or shallow cake tins and place a pizza base in each, forming a rim around the edge.

● **Step 5** Brush the dough with oil and spread with tomato sauce. Top with the mozzarella. Drizzle with a little oil. Bake for 15–20 minutes until golden. Serve hot, garnished with whole fresh basil leaves.

Calories per portion 900 Kcal ● Fat per portion 43.2g ● Serves 4

Step 2 *Add the dried thyme to the tomatoes in the pan and simmer for 2 minutes. Season and add the basil.*

Step 3 *Roll out each piece of dough on a lightly floured surface to a 20cm (8in) round.*

Step 5 *Top the pizza bases with tomato sauce and sliced mozzarella. Drizzle with olive oil and bake.*

✔ *Easy*   ❄ *Freeze it*

Spaghetti Bolognese

Preparation time 5 minutes ● Cooking time 40 minutes

400g (14oz) minced beef

1 large onion, chopped

2 garlic cloves, crushed

2 x 400g cans chopped tomatoes

1 tablespoon tomato purée

1 teaspoon each dried basil and
  oregano

2 teaspoons sugar

125ml glass red wine

Salt and freshly ground black pepper

12 olives, chopped

250g (9oz) spaghetti

● **1** Place the minced beef in a large pan and cook over a medium heat until well browned. Drain off any excess fat, then add the onion and garlic and cook, stirring, for 2–3 minutes.

● **2** Add the tomatoes, purée, basil, oregano, sugar and wine and bring to the boil. Season and simmer for 20–30 minutes until the sauce has thickened.

● **3** Meanwhile, cook the spaghetti in a pan of boiling salted water according to the pack instructions until tender. Drain well. Add the chopped olives to the sauce and serve with the spaghetti.

Calories per portion 524 Kcal ● Fat per portion 19g ● Serves 4

Serve with...

Serve the pasta and sauce topped with chopped fresh parsley and a sprinkling of grated Parmesan cheese if you like.

Why not try...

Make up a large batch of sauce and freeze individual portions for quick and easy midweek suppers.

✎ Make it spicy...

Add a large pinch of dried chilli flakes to the sauce in step 2 for an extra kick.

🕐 *Super Quick* ✓✓ *Extra Easy* Ⓝ *Contains Nuts*

Pesto Prawn Spaghetti

Preparation time 5 minutes ● Cooking time 10 minutes

1 tablespoon olive oil

1 onion, chopped

2 garlic cloves, crushed

350g (12oz) raw tiger prawns, peeled

2 tablespoons pine nuts, toasted

Zest and juice of ½ lemon

2 tablespoons green pesto

1 tablespoon capers, chopped

250g (9oz) spaghetti

● **1** Cook the spaghetti in a pan of boiling water according to the packet instructions until tender. Drain well.

● **2** Meanwhile, heat the oil in a frying pan. Add the onion and garlic and fry for 2 minutes, then add the prawns and cook briefly until pink. Add the pine nuts, lemon zest and juice, pesto and capers. Mix well to combine. Add to the cooked pasta and toss together.

Calories per portion 378 Kcal ● Fat per portion 9.9g ● Serves 4

Serve with…

Just add some fresh crusty bread for a quick and easy midweek meal.

Why not try…

You could use frozen mixed seafood instead of the prawns if you prefer. Just cook until piping hot.

Sausage & Sage Pasta

Preparation time 10 minutes ● Cooking time 20 minutes

400g (14oz) short pasta

1 tablespoon olive oil

1 onion, sliced

2 garlic cloves, crushed

4 low-fat sausages, skinned and
    crumbled

2 x 400g cans chopped tomatoes

3 fresh sage leaves, chopped

Worcestershire sauce, optional

Salt and freshly ground pepper

● **1** Cook the pasta in a pan of boiling, salted water according to the pack instructions until tender.

● **2** Meanwhile, heat the oil in a frying pan and cook the onions and garlic over a medium heat, stirring occasionally. Add the sausages and stir to break up the meat. Cook for about 5 minutes until browned.

● **3** Add the tomatoes and sage. Simmer for 10 minutes, stirring occasionally. Season with salt, pepper and a dash of Worcestershire sauce, if using. Drain the pasta and return to the pan. Add the sauce and toss together.

Calories per portion 500 Kcal ● Fat per portion 10g ● Serves 4

Serve with...

This dish makes a meal by itself or you can serve it with a simple green salad.

🌿 Make it spicy...

Use spicy sausages for an extra flavour boost and add a pinch of chilli flakes or chilli powder to the sauce.

● *Quick* ✓✓ *Extra Easy*

Quick Parma Ham Pizza

Preparation time 10 minutes ● Cooking time 15 minutes

265g jar tomato pizza sauce

1 ready-made thin crust pizza base

2 x 125g mozzarella balls, drained

   and chopped or grated

1 onion, chopped

6 slices Parma ham, cut into ribbons

Olive oil, to drizzle

¼ teaspoon paprika

½ teaspoon each dried thyme and

   oregano

2 handfuls rocket leaves

40g (1½oz) Parmesan, grated

● **1** Preheat the oven to 190°C/375°F/Gas 5. Spread a generous layer of tomato sauce across the pizza base. Sprinkle over the mozzarella and chopped onion, then arrange the Parma ham on top.

● **2** Drizzle with a little olive oil and season with paprika, oregano and thyme. Bake on the oven shelf for 10 minutes. Top with the rocket and Parmesan. Cook for a further 5 minutes until the base begins to crisp.

Calories per portion 424 Kcal ● Fat per portion 25.9g ● Serves 4

Serve with...

Serve with extra rocket leaves tossed with Parmesan shavings and drizzled with a little olive oil.

🕐 *Super Quick* ✓✓ *Extra Easy*

Creamy Salmon Tagliatelle

Preparation time 5 minutes ● Cooking time 10 minutes

400g (14oz) tagliatelle

Salt and freshly ground black pepper

2 x 120g packs smoked salmon
   trimmings

142ml pot double cream

150g pot low-fat Greek yogurt

Juice of ½ lemon

Chopped fresh dill, to garnish

● **1** Cook the tagliatelle in a pan of boiling salted water according to the pack instructions until tender. Drain and return to the pan.

● **2** Meanwhile, chop the smoked salmon trimmings and mix with the cream, yogurt, lemon juice and salt and black pepper.

● **3** Add the salmon mixture to the tagliatelle and toss together until well combined. Season and serve garnished with lots of chopped fresh dill.

Calories per portion 635 Kcal ● Fat per portion 24.3g ● Serves 4

Serve with...
**Serve this simple dish with buttered
soda bread on the side.**

🕐 *Make it at the Weekend*   Ⓥ *Vegetarian*

Macaroni Cheese Pie

Preparation time 20 minutes plus resting ● Cooking time 45 minutes

450g (1lb) puff pastry

2 x 350g tubs cheese sauce

40g (1½oz) freshly grated Parmesan

2 tablespoons crème fraîche

Squeeze of lemon juice

Salt and freshly ground black pepper

75g (3oz) macaroni, cooked

25g (1oz) butter

125g (4oz) button mushrooms, sliced

200g (7oz) canned artichoke hearts,
   drained and sliced

125g (4oz) hollandaise sauce

2 tablespoons softly whipped cream

● **Step 1** Preheat the oven to 200C/400F/Gas 6. Place 4 x deep 10cm (4in) metal cooking rings on a baking tray. Roll out the pastry. Cut out 4 x 10cm (4in) circles and place in the base of the rings. Cut the remaining pastry into wide strips to line the sides. Press the edges together to seal the base.

● **2** Line the pastry with greaseproof paper and fill with dried beans. Rest in the fridge for 20 minutes. Bake for 10–15 minutes. Remove the paper and beans. Bake for another 10 minutes. Carefully remove the rings.

● **Step 3** Heat 1 tub of cheese sauce in a large pan until hot. Stir in the Parmesan and creme fraiche until melted. Add the lemon juice, season and stir in the macaroni. Heat gently until warmed through.

● **4** Melt the butter in a pan and fry the mushrooms for 5 minutes until soft. Add to the macaroni with the artichokes. Spoon into the pastry cases.

● **Step 5** Preheat the grill to high. Warm the remaining sauce and stir in the hollandaise and cream. Spoon into the pies, levelling the tops with the back of the spoon. Grill until the topping is dark golden.

Calories per portion 1107 Kcal ● Fat per portion 81g ● Serves 4

Step 1 *Line the cooking rings with puff pastry, making sure it comes up higher than the side of the rings.*

Step 3 *Add the cooked macaroni to the pan of Parmesan cheese sauce and stir until heated through.*

Step 5 *Spoon the Cheddar cheese sauce over the tops of the pies and spread level with the back of the spoon.*

● *Quick* ✓✓ *Extra Easy* 🌶 *Spicy* Ⓥ *Vegetarian*

Ricotta Pizza

Preparation time 10 minutes ● Cooking time 15 minutes

250g tub ricotta

Salt and freshly ground black pepper

2 x 20cm (8in) ready-made pizza
  bases

12 plum tomatoes, cut into wedges

Pinch dried chilli flakes

Handful fresh basil leaves, torn

Extra virgin olive oil or chilli oil, to
  serve

● **1** Preheat the oven to 200°C/400°F/Gas 6. Season the ricotta with salt and black pepper, then spread over the pizza bases. Top with tomato wedges, then sprinkle with the chilli flakes, if using.

● **2** Bake for 10–15 minutes until the tomatoes are soft. Scatter with torn basil leaves and drizzle with a little olive or chilli oil just before serving.

Calories per portion 460 Kcal ● Fat per portion 14g ● Serves 4

Serve with...

A simple salad of baby spinach and rocket leaves would go well with this rich pizza.

Why not try...

You could add some sliced black olives to the topping for an extra Mediterranean flavour.

✓ *Easy*   🌶 *Spicy*   Ⓥ *Vegetarian*

Sweet & Sour Pepper Pasta

Preparation time 10 minutes ● Cooking time 30 minutes

300g (11oz) fusilli

Salt and freshly ground black pepper

1 tablespoon olive oil

1 garlic clove, crushed

1 red onion, finely sliced

2 red peppers, deseeded and roughly
    chopped

1 yellow pepper, deseeded and
    roughly chopped

1 red chilli, finely chopped

500g carton passata

2 tablespoons white wine vinegar

2 teaspoons caster sugar

● **1** Cook the pasta in a pan of boiling salted water according to the pack instructions until tender. Meanwhile, heat the oil in a large, non-stick pan and fry the garlic and onion for 2 minutes. Add the red and yellow peppers and the chilli and fry for 5 minutes.

● **2** Add the passata, vinegar and sugar and stir until the sugar has dissolved. Season. Simmer over a low heat for 15–20 minutes until the peppers are tender. If sauce becomes too thick, add a little water. Drain the pasta and add to the sauce. Mix well and serve immediately.

Calories per portion 265 Kcal ● Fat per portion 5g ● Serves 4

Serve with...

Serve this flavoursome pasta dish with slices of French bread rubbed with a cut garlic clove and toasted.

Why not try...

You can use any short pasta shapes for this dish, such as penne or conchiglie.

Salmon & Spinach Lasagne

Preparation time 40 minutes ● Cooking time 45 minutes

700g (1½lb) fresh spinach

2 tablespoons olive oil

550g (1¼lb) salmon fillet

21 sheets egg lasagne

12 sprigs each fresh chervil and
    flat-leaf parsley, finely chopped

175g (6oz) Parmesan, grated

25g (1oz) butter, diced

For the sauce

50g (2oz) butter

25g (1oz) flour

300ml (½pt) milk

200ml (7fl oz) single cream

Pinch grated nutmeg

Salt and freshly ground black pepper

40g (1½oz) Parmesan, grated

● **1** Place the spinach in a pan with the oil and 2 tablespoons water. Cook for 5 minutes until wilted and all the liquid has evaporated. Set aside.

● **2** To make the sauce, melt the butter in a pan over a low heat, add the flour and stir for 1–2 minutes to make a smooth paste. Gradually stir in the milk and cream and bring to the boil, stirring. Reduce the heat and stir until the sauce begins to thicken. Add a pinch of nutmeg and some black pepper.

● **3** Simmer for 10 minutes over a low heat, stirring occasionally. If the sauce gets too thick, add a little milk. Stir in the Parmesan until melted. Chop the salmon and place in a bowl. Add 4 tablespoons of the sauce and season.

● **4** Cook the lasagne in a large pan of boiling salted water until just starting to soften. Drain and spread out the sheets on a clean tea towel. Preheat the oven to 200°C/400°F/Gas 6 and grease a large baking dish.

● **5** Spoon a thin layer of sauce into the dish then add a double layer of lasagne. Top with a layer of salmon, then spread all the spinach on top. Add another layer of lasagne and sauce then sprinkle with herbs and Parmesan.

● **6** Continue with layers of pasta, salmon, pasta and finish with sauce and chopped herbs. Sprinkle over the butter and remaining Parmesan. Bake for 25 minutes until piping hot.

Calories per portion 826 Kcal ● Fat per portion 45.5g ● Serves 6

Serve with…

**Serve the lasagne with a sprig of chervil
and a warm focaccia or ciabatta loaf.**

Easy

Seafood Pasta

Preparation time 10 minutes ● Cooking time 25 minutes

400g (14oz) pasta shells

Low-fat cooking spray

1 large onion, chopped

1 large bulb fennel, chopped

1 garlic clove, crushed

400g can chopped tomatoes

350g bag frozen mixed seafood

2 tablespoons chopped fresh parsley

● **1** Cook the pasta in a pan of boiling water according to the pack instructions until tender. Meanwhile, spray a frying pan with cooking spray and heat until hot. Stir-fry the onion, fennel and garlic until softened.

● **2** Add the chopped tomatoes and a can of hot water. Bring to the boil, reduce the heat and simmer for 15 minutes. Stir in the seafood and parsley. Cook until heated through. Drain the pasta and toss with the sauce.

Calories per portion 456 Kcal ● Fat per portion 3.6g ● Serves 4

Serve with...

Simply serve with some fresh wholemeal bread for a hearty meal.

 *Make it spicy...*

Add a chopped red chilli to the pan with the onion and fennel in step 1.

Easy

Sausage & Red Pepper Pizza

Preparation time 10 minutes ● Cooking time 25 minutes

290g pack pizza dough mix

6 tablespoons passata

50g (2oz) Cheddar, grated

4 sausages, skins removed, meat
  crumbled

1 red pepper, deseeded and sliced

Freshly ground black pepper

1 tablespoon olive oil

● **1** Preheat the oven to 200°C/400F/Gas 6. Make up the pizza dough mix according to the pack instructions. Roll out to a 30 x 23cm (12 x 9in) and place on a lightly oiled baking tray.

● **2** Spread the base with passata and top with Cheddar, pieces of sausage and pepper slices. Season with freshly ground black pepper and drizzle with oil. Bake for 20–25 minutes until the dough is golden and crisp.

Calories per portion 425 Kcal ● Fat per portion 19g ● Serves 4

Serve with...

Serve this tasty pizza with a rocket salad drizzled with balsamic dressing.

Why not try...

You could add griddled steak strips or some spicy chorizo sausage if you like.

Pasta with Steak & Olives

Preparation time 5 minutes ● Cooking time 15 minutes

400g (14oz) short pasta

Salt and freshly ground black pepper

400g (14oz) rump steak

1 teaspoon olive oil

2 x 400g cans chopped tomatoes

with garlic

2 tablespoons roughly chopped fresh

oregano

4 tablespoons pitted green olives,

halved

1 Preheat the grill to high. Cook the pasta in a pan of boiling salted water according to the pack instructions until tender. Meanwhile, brush the steak with oil, season with freshly ground black pepper and grill for 3 minutes on each side, or until cooked to your liking. Set aside.

2 Heat the tomatoes in a pan with the oregano and olives, then season with salt and pepper. Thinly slice the steak and add to the tomato sauce. Drain the pasta and return to the pan. Add the sauce and toss to mix.

Calories per portion 530 Kcal ● Fat per portion 9.5g ● Serves 4

Serve with...

Sliced warm ciabatta or focaccia loaf would go well with this meaty dish.

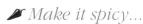 *Make it spicy...*

Use canned tomatoes with added chilli or stir in a dash of Tabasco sauce.

Prawn & Tomato Pasta

Preparation time 5 minutes ● Cooking time 15 minutes

400g (14oz) long pasta, eg spaghetti,

linguine or tagliatelle

Salt and freshly ground black pepper

1 tablespoon olive oil

2 x 250g tubs cherry tomatoes,

halved

2 garlic cloves, crushed

300g (11oz) cooked prawns

1 teaspoon dried chilli flakes

2 tablespoons roughly chopped fresh

parsley

● **1** Cook the pasta in a pan of boiling salted water according to the pack instructions until tender. Meanwhile, heat the oil in a frying pan and cook the tomatoes and garlic for 5 minutes.

● **2** Add the prawns and season with salt, pepper, and chilli. Cook for 3–5 minutes until the prawns are heated through. Drain the pasta and return to the pan. Stir in the sauce, add the parsley and serve immediately.

Calories per portion 461 Kcal ● Fat per portion 6g ● Serves 4

Serve with...

Serve on its own or with some crusty bread to mop up the sauce.

● *Quick* ✓✓ *Extra Easy*

Simple Tuna Spaghetti

Preparation time 5 minutes ● Cooking time 15 minutes

400g (14oz) spaghetti or linguine

Salt and freshly ground black pepper

6–8 tomatoes, roughly chopped

2 x 185g cans tuna in brine, drained

2–3 teaspoons balsamic vinegar

● **1** Cook the spaghetti in a pan of boiling salted water according to the pack instructions until tender. Drain well and return to the pan. Add the tomatoes and tuna and toss over the heat until well mixed and heated through. Add balsamic vinegar to taste and season with salt and pepper.

Calories per portion 440 Kcal ● Fat per portion 2.6g ● Serves 4

Serve with...

Serve with a mixed salad or some fresh bread and butter

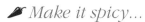 *Make it spicy...*

If you like a hot dish, season with Tabasco or sweet chilli sauce instead of the balsamic vinegar.

Quick ✓ *Easy*

Pizza Fiorentina

Preparation time 10 minutes ● Cooking time 20 minutes

23cm (9in) ready-made pizza base

5 tablespoons passata

50g (2oz) spinach, cooked and
  drained

3 wafer-thin slices ham, halved

50g (2oz) mozzarella, diced

25g (1oz) Parmesan, grated

2 tablespoons olive oil

1–2 garlic cloves, finely chopped

½ teaspoon dried oregano

Salt and freshly ground black pepper

1 egg

● **1** Preheat the oven to 220°C/425F/Gas 7. Cover the pizza base with passata, then top with spinach and ham. Add the mozzarella, then sprinkle with grated Parmesan, oil, garlic and oregano. Season. Cook for 10 minutes.

● **2** Make a small well in the centre and gently break in the egg. Return to the oven and cook for a further 5–10 minutes until the egg is cooked through.

Calories per portion 460 Kcal ● Fat per portion 22g ● Serves 1

Serve with...

**This tasty pizza makes a hearty supper
for one. If you want to share it, break
2 eggs on top instead of 1.**

Stuffed Pasta Shells

Preparation time 25 minutes ● Cooking time 20 minutes

32 large conchiglie shells

250g (9oz) frozen edamame (soya

   beans) or broad beans

150g (5oz) fresh or frozen peas

14 asparagus spears

300g (11oz) ricotta

2 teaspoons olive oil

Large pinch dried mixed herbs

Salt and freshly ground black pepper

● **1** Cook the pasta shells in a pan of boiling water according to the pack instructions until tender. Drain and rinse in boiling water. Meanwhile, cook the beans and peas in a pan of boiling water until tender and the asparagus in another pan of water until tender but still firm. Drain the vegetables.

● **2** Chop 2 asparagus spears and place in a pan with three-quarters of the peas and beans. Mix in the ricotta and mixed herbs. Season with salt and black pepper and heat gently until well combined.

● **3** Spoon the mixture into the pasta shells and place in a dish. Scatter over the remaining peas, beans and asparagus and drizzle with olive oil. Serve.

Calories per portion 608 Kcal ● Fat per portion 15.4g ● Serves 4

Serve with...

Serve this fresh summer dish with a mixed green salad and ciabatta bread.

Why not try...

For an extra crunch, fry some wholemeal breadcrumbs in butter until golden and crisp. Mix with crumbled crispy bacon and scatter over the dish.

Baked Ravioli

Preparation time 5 minutes ● Cooking time 40 minutes

1 aubergine, sliced into 5mm (½in) rounds

Olive oil, for brushing

2 x 300g packs filled ravioli, such as wild mushroom

2 x 250g packs cherry tomatoes, halved

200ml (7fl oz) hot vegetable stock

2 tablespoons chopped fresh parsley

1 Preheat the oven to 180°C/350°F/Gas 4. Brush the aubergine slices with olive oil. Heat a frying pan over a medium heat and fry the aubergines, in 2 or 3 batches until browned. Drain on kitchen paper.

2 Drizzle a large ovenproof dish with oil. Add the pasta, tomatoes and fried aubergines, mixing them evenly. Pour over the stock. Cover the dish with foil and bake for 20 minutes until the tomatoes have started to break down.

3 Remove the foil and bake for a further 5 minutes until the pasta is tender and lightly golden. Sprinkle with parsley and serve.

Calories per portion 290 Kcal ● Fat per portion 12g ● Serves 4

Serve with...

This dish makes a delicious meal on its own or served with fresh crusty bread and a mixed leaf salad.

Why not try...

This dish is suitable for vegetarians but you can choose a meat-filled pasta instead if you prefer.

Quick ✓ *Easy*

Linguine with Scallops

Preparation time 10 minutes ● Cooking time 15 minutes

1 tablespoon olive oil

2 leeks, finely chopped

2 garlic cloves, finely chopped

200g (7oz) linguine

4–6 scallops, with or without roe,
  halved or quartered, if large

4 tablespoons dry white wine

4 tablespoons vegetable stock

Bunch rocket leaves

Flat-leaf parsley to garnish

● **1** Heat the oil in a large, heavy-based frying pan and cook the leeks gently for 5–10 minutes until softened. Add the garlic and cook for 2 minutes.

● **2** Meanwhile, cook the linguine in a large pan of boiling, salted water according to the pack instructions. Drain and return to the pan with a little of the cooking water.

● **3** Add the scallops to the leeks and cook for 1 minute each side. Pour in the wine and stock and bring to the boil. Reduce to a simmer and cook for 5 minutes. Remove from the heat, stir in the rocket and season. Add to the pasta and toss together. Serve with a sprinkling of parsley.

Calories per portion 485 Kcal ● Fat per portion 8g ● Serves 2

Serve with...

This sophisticated dinner for two doesn't need any accompaniment apart from some sliced French bread.

Why not try...

You could add some chopped crispy bacon or cooked peas to the dish.

Make it at the Weekend ✓ *Easy* 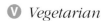 *Vegetarian*

Spinach & Four Cheese Shells

Preparation time 20 minutes ● Cooking time 35 minutes

18 large pasta shells

Salt and freshly ground black pepper

Low-fat cooking spray

1 onion, finely chopped

2 garlic cloves, crushed

225g (8oz) spinach

150g (5oz) ricotta

250g (9oz) Quark (very low-fat

   soft cheese)

25g (1oz) freshly grated Parmesan

Pinch freshly grated nutmeg

700g jar passata

125g (4oz) light mozzarella, drained

   and diced

1 tablespoon shredded fresh basil,

   plus extra leaves, to serve

1 Preheat the oven to 190°C/375F/Gas 5. Cook the pasta shells in a pan of boiling salted water according to the packet instructions until tender. Drain.

2 Heat some low-fat cooking spray in a pan, add the onion and cook for 5 minutes until softened. Add the garlic and spinach, cover the pan and cook for 5 minutes, stirring occasionally, until the spinach has wilted.

3 Tip the spinach mixture into a bowl and leave to cool slightly. Stir in the ricotta, Quark, half the Parmesan and the nutmeg. Season to taste. Spoon into the pasta shells.

4 Pour a quarter of the passata over the base of an ovenproof dish. Tuck the filled shells into the dish and scatter the mozzarella over the top. Pour over the remaining passata, then scatter over the basil and remaining Parmesan. Bake for 25 minutes until hot and bubbling. Serve garnished with basil.

Calories per portion 465 Kcal ● Fat per portion 8.4g ● Serves 6

Serve with…

A salad of sliced tomatoes drizzled with olive oil and seasoned with salt and pepper goes well with this meal.

Quick ✓✓ *Extra Easy*

Tuna Pasta Salad

Preparation time 10 minutes ● Cooking time 10 minutes

300g (11oz) pasta spirals

Salt and freshly ground black pepper

Low-fat cooking spray

3 mixed peppers, deseeded and
   sliced

200g can sweetcorn kernels, drained

2 x 185g cans tuna in brine, drained

4–5 tablespoons fat-free salad
   dressing

3 tablespoons chopped fresh parsley

1 Cook the pasta in a pan of boiling salted water according to the pack instructions until tender. Drain and rinse under cold running water to cool.

2 Meanwhile, spray a frying pan with a little cooking spray and fry the peppers for 3–4 minutes until just starting to soften. Remove from the pan.

3 Mix together the sweetcorn, tuna and peppers and toss with the pasta until well combined. Add the salad dressing, parsley and season to taste.

Calories per portion 426 Kcal ● Fat per portion 3.1g ● Serves 4

Serve with...

Serve this cold pasta dish with some mixed salad leaves and pitta breads.

✎ *Make it spicy...*

Choose a salad dressing with added chilli for a spicy kick.

🕐 *Quick* ✓✓ *Extra Easy* Ⓥ *Vegetarian*

Antipasti Pizza

Preparation time 5 minutes ● Cooking time 15 minutes

2 x 23cm (9in) pizza bases

250g tub mascarpone

100g (3½oz) grilled mushrooms,
   halved

100g (3½oz) olives, roughly chopped

125g (4oz) sunblush tomatoes

Freshly ground black pepper

2 tablespoons olive oil

2 handfuls rocket leaves

● **1** Preheat the oven to 200°C/400°F/Gas 6. Spread the pizza bases with mascarpone. Top with the mushrooms, olives and tomatoes. Season with black pepper. Place on a baking sheet and cook for 10–15 minutes until golden. Drizzle with oil, scatter with the rocket leaves and serve.

Calories per portion 684 Kcal ● Fat per portion 55g ● Serves 4

Serve with...

These pizzas make a perfect lunch on their own or served with extra salad.

Why not try...

Choose your favourite ingredients from the deli counter, such as grilled aubergines, mini mozzarella balls, artichoke hearts or thinly sliced salami or Parma ham.

🕐 *Quick* ✓✓ *Extra Easy* Ⓥ *Vegetarian*

Creamy Mushroom Pasta

Preparation time 5 minutes ● Cooking time 15 minutes

400g (14oz) ribbon pasta, eg
 pappardelle or tagliatelle

Salt and freshly ground black pepper

1 tablespoon olive oil

450g (1lb) mixed wild mushrooms,
 sliced

2 garlic cloves, crushed

2 tablespoons white wine or brandy

100g (3½oz) reduced-fat crème
 fraîche

2 tablespoons roughly chopped fresh
 parsley

● **1** Cook the pasta in a pan of boiling salted water according to the pack instructions until tender. Meanwhile, heat the oil in a non-stick frying pan and cook the mushrooms and garlic for 5 minutes.

● **2** Add the wine or brandy and simmer for 1 minute. Stir in the crème fraîche and parsley and season with salt and black pepper. Drain the pasta and return to the pan. Add the sauce and stir to combine.

Calories per portion 450 Kcal ● Fat per portion 9g ● Serves 4

Serve with…
**Serve the pasta with toasted granary
bread and rocket salad.**

Turkey & Tomato Pasta

Preparation time 5 minutes ● Cooking time 10 minutes

300g (11oz) penne

Salt

Low-fat cooking spray

300g (11oz) turkey fillet, chopped

1 quantity Classic Tomato Sauce (see

    page 11) or 350g jar chunky

    tomato pasta sauce

40g (1½oz) finely grated Parmesan

Dash Tabasco sauce

● **1** Cook the pasta in a pan of boiling salted water according to the pack instructions until tender. Meanwhile, spray a non-stick frying pan with a little cooking spray and fry the turkey until cooked through.

● **2** Drain the pasta and return to the pan. Add the turkey, tomato sauce, Parmesan and Tabasco sauce to taste. Stir over a low heat until warmed through and the Parmesan has melted. Serve immediately.

Calories per portion 440 Kcal ● Fat per portion 10.1g ● Serves 4

Serve with...

Serve the pasta with a salad of mixed leaves tossed with a little fat-free dressing of your choice.

Salmon & Herb Pasta

Preparation time 5 minutes ● Cooking time 10 minutes

300g (11oz) tagliatelle

Salt and freshly ground black pepper

1 tablespoon olive oil

3 spring onions, finely sliced

200ml tub crème fraîche

200g (7oz) smoked salmon, roughly
   chopped

1 tablespoon chopped mixed fresh
   herbs, such as dill, flat-leaf parsley,
   coriander, chives

Zest and juice of 1 lemon

● **1** Cook the pasta in a pan of boiling salted water according to the packet instructions. Meanwhile, gently heat the oil in a medium pan. Add the spring onions and cook for 1–2 minutes to soften.

● **2** Stir in the crème fraiche until warmed through. Fold in the salmon and herbs and season with black pepper, lemon zest and juice. Drain the pasta, stir in the sauce until combined and serve.

Calories per portion 382Kcal ● Fat per portion 22g ● Serves 4

Serve with...

**Buttered brown bread makes the ideal
accompaniment to this simple dish.**

Quick ✓✓ *Extra Easy* Ⓥ *Vegetarian*

Roasted Tomato & Olive Pasta

Preparation time 5 minutes ● Cooking time 15 minutes

500g pack baby plum tomatoes

2 tablespoons olive oil

350g (12oz) spaghetti

16 black olives, pitted and halved

4 tablespoons chopped fresh flat-leaf

    parsley

Salt and freshly ground black pepper

● **1** Preheat the oven to 200°C/400°F/Gas 6. Place the tomatoes in a roasting tin, drizzle with oil and roast for 15 minutes until soft and lightly charred.

● **2** Meanwhile, cook the pasta in a pan of boiling salted water according to the pack instructions until tender, then drain. Add the tomatoes, olives, and parsley and toss together. Season with salt and black pepper and serve.

Calories per portion 384 Kcal ● Fat per portion 9g ● Serves 4

Serve with...

**This simple supper goes beautifully
with some crusty French bread.**

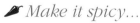 *Make it spicy...*

**Add a pinch of chilli flakes or a diced
and lightly cooked red chilli to the pasta
for an extra boost of heat.**

● *Make it at the Weekend* ⓝ *Contains Nuts* ⓥ *Vegetarian*

Spinach & Ricotta Cannelloni

Preparation time 20 minutes ● Cooking time 50 minutes

200g (7oz) ricotta

1 garlic clove, crushed

3 eggs

Salt and freshly ground black pepper

2 tablespoons pine nuts, toasted

400g (14oz) spinach

16 cannelloni tubes

100ml (4fl oz) cream (30% fat)

125g (4oz) Parmesan, grated

2 tablespoons ice-cold butter, diced

● **Step 1** Mix together the ricotta, garlic and 1 egg and season with salt and black pepper. Roughly chop the pine nuts and stir in.

● **2** Cook the spinach in a little boiling, salted water until wilted. Drain, refresh in cold water and drain well. Squeeze out as much liquid as you can with your hands and chop roughly.

● **Step 3** Stir the spinach into the ricotta mixture, then spoon the mixture into a piping bag fitted with a plain nozzle. Pipe into the cannelloni tubes.

● **Step 4** Grease 4 small (or 1 large) baking dishes and add the cannelloni tubes. Whisk the cream with the remaining eggs and season with salt and pepper. Pour over the cannelloni. Sprinkle with Parmesan and dot with butter. Bake for 40–45 minutes until golden and bubbling.

Calories per portion 820 Kcal ● Fat per portion 42g ● Serves 4

Step 1 *Roughly chop the toasted pine nuts and stir into the ricotta mixture until well combined.*

Step 3 *Spoon the ricotta mixture into a piping bag and fill the cannelloni tubes, or push in with a teaspoon.*

Step 4 *Pour the cream mixture over the cannelloni then scatter over the Parmesan and dot with butter.*

Easy

Sausage & Artichoke Pasta

Preparation time 15 minutes ● Cooking time 25 minutes

Drizzle olive oil

1 red onion, finely chopped

Salt and freshly ground black pepper

6 good-quality sausages, skinned

1 small glass white wine

2 garlic cloves, finely chopped

½ x 400g jar artichokes, roughly
    chopped

Handful pitted black olives, chopped

Handful fresh parsley, finely chopped

142ml carton double cream

450g (1lb) rigatoni

Grated fresh Parmesan, to serve

● **1** Heat the oil in a large frying pan, add the onion and season. Cook gently until soft, then add the sausage meat and chop with the back of a fork. Cook and mash until no longer pink and the mixture has broken down.

● **2** Increase the heat and add the white wine. Bubble for a few minutes until the wine evaporates, then stir in the garlic, artichokes and olives. Cook for 5–10 minutes, stirring occasionally. Add the parsley and cream and cook for a further 5 minutes.

● **3** Meanwhile, cook the pasta in a pan of boiling salted water according to the pack instructions until tender. Drain and return to the pan with a little of the cooking water. Toss with the sauce and top with grated Parmesan.

Calories per portion 852 Kcal ● Fat per portion 43g ● Serves 4

Serve with…

Serve with some crisp breadsticks and extra olives if you like.

Make it spicy…

Use spicy sausages, such as chorizo or merguez for extra flavour.

● *Quick* ✓ *Easy* Ⓥ *Vegetarian*

Smoked Cheese Macaroni

Preparation time 10 minutes ● Cooking time 15 minutes

225g (8oz) frozen peas

350g (12oz) macaroni

Salt and freshly ground black pepper

Knob of butter

1 tablespoon plain flour

450ml (¾pt) milk

1 teaspoon English mustard

150g pack smoked cheese

3–4 spring onions, finely chopped

Grated Cheddar, for topping,
    optional

● **1** Place the peas in a dish and cover with boiling water. Leave for 5 minutes, then drain and set aside. Cook the macaroni in a pan of boiling salted water according to the pack instructions until tender. Drain and return to the pan.

● **2** Meanwhile, make the cheese sauce. Melt the butter in a pan, then stir in the flour and cook for 1 minute, stirring. Remove from the heat and add the remaining milk. Return to the heat and cook, stirring, until boiling and thickened. Add the mustard and smoked cheese and stir until melted.

● **3** Preheat the grill to high. Mix together the pasta and sauce, then tip in the peas and stir in the spring onions and seasoning. Transfer to an ovenproof dish and grate Cheddar on top, if using. Grill until the top is golden.

Calories per portion 600 Kcal ● Fat per portion 21g ● Serves 4

Serve with...

A green salad and garlic bread would go well with this vegetarian dish.

Why not try...

For a meaty version, add crispy bacon or cooked chicken. Fried mushrooms and wilted spinach leaves would also make good additions.

Spinach & Ham Calzone

Preparation time 15 minutes plus rising ● Cooking time 10 minutes

½ x 500g pack ciabatta bread mix

½ tablespoon olive oil

400g can plum tomatoes

Salt and freshly ground black pepper

250g bag spinach, washed

4 slices cooked ham, torn

125g pack mozzarella, drained
   and torn

Pinch dried oregano

Handful capers (optional)

1 Preheat the oven to 200°C/400°F/Gas 6. Tip the ciabatta mix into a bowl along with 175ml (6fl oz) warm water. Mix to form a smooth dough, then add the olive oil and mix again. Cover with a damp tea towel and leave to rise for 15–20 minutes.

2 Cut the dough in half and roll out each half to make a thin round. Transfer to a large oiled baking tray.

3 Place the tomatoes in a large bowl, season with salt and black pepper, and whizz until smooth with a hand blender. Spread a thin layer of sauce over half of each dough circle, reserving a little for later.

4 Arrange the spinach, ham and most of the cheese on top of the sauce. Fold over the dough and pinch the edges to secure. Spread the remaining sauce on top, add the remaining mozzarella and sprinkle with oregano and capers, if using. Bake for 8–10 minutes until risen and beginning to brown.

Calories per portion 732 Kcal ● Fat per portion 19g ● Serves 2

Serve with...
Serve the calzone with mixed leaf salad drizzled with vinaigrette dressing.

Why not try...
Use tomato passata instead of blitzing the canned tomatoes if you prefer.

✎ Make it spicy...
Add a pinch of dried chilli flakes or hot chilli powder to the tomato sauce.

🕐 *Quick* ✓ *Easy* Ⓥ *Vegetarian*

Tricolour Pasta Salad

Preparation time 15 minutes ● Cooking time 15 minutes

1 small head broccoli, cut into small
   florets

Salt and freshly ground black pepper

3 tablespoons olive oil

2 courgettes, 1 sliced, 1 cut into thin
   ribbons

15 small radishes, quartered

198g can sweetcorn, drained

250g (9oz) multi-colour pasta twists

Balsamic vinegar, to drizzle

Few sprigs flat-leaf parsley, chopped

● **1** Cook the broccoli in a pan of boiling lightly salted water for 5–7 minutes until tender but not soft. Drain and rinse with cold water to cool.

● **2** Heat 2 tablespoons oil in a large frying pan. Add the courgettes, salt and pepper and radishes and cook until tender but not soft. Add the sweetcorn and broccoli, stir well and remove from the heat. Meanwhile, cook the pasta in a pan of boiling water according to the pack instructions until tender.

● **3** Drain the pasta, rinse under cold water and add to the vegetables. Pour into a large salad bowl. Drizzle over the remaining olive oil and and a little balsamic vinegar and garnish with chopped parsley.

Calories per portion 385 Kcal ● Fat per portion 10.9g ● Serves 4

Serve with...
This salad is a perfect light lunch on its own and is also great served alongside a barbecue or as part of a buffet.

Why not try...
You can vary the vegetables to suit what you have available. Frozen peas, canned chickpeas, carrot ribbons and sliced peppers all work well.

✓✓ Extra Easy ⓥ *Vegetarian*

Penne with Pumpkin & Sage

Preparation time 10 minutes ● Cooking time 30 minutes

1 small pumpkin, deseeded, peeled
   and diced (about 1kg/2lb 3oz
   prepared weight)

4 tablespoons olive oil

20 fresh sage leaves

2 garlic cloves, crushed

500g pack penne

50g (2oz) butter, melted

8 tablespoons grated Parmesan

Salt and freshly ground black pepper

● **1** Preheat the oven to 200°C/400°F/Gas 6. Place the pumpkin in a roasting tin, drizzle with 2 tablespoons oil and roast for 20 minutes. Add the sage leaves and garlic and cook for a further 5–10 minutes until tender.

● **2** Meanwhile, cook the pasta in a pan of boiling water according to the pack instructions until tender, then drain and return to the pan. Add the butter, remaining oil and the roast pumpkin, sage and garlic. Season with salt and pepper, stir together and serve sprinkled with grated Parmesan.

Calories per portion 743 Kcal ● Fat per portion 31g ● Serves 4

Serve with...

This dish makes a hearty supper on its own or served with salad and bread.

Why not try...

If you can't find pumpkin, use butternut squash instead. You will need the same prepared weight – 1kg (2lb 3oz).

Bacon & Tomato Pasta Bake

Preparation time 5 minutes ● Cooking time 30 minutes

300g (11oz) penne

200g pack bacon bits

200g jar sun-dried tomatoes, drained
    and roughly chopped

350g jar four-cheese pasta sauce

25g (1oz) white breadcrumbs

50g (2oz) Cheddar or Parmesan,
    grated

2 tablespoons roughly chopped fresh
    parsley

Zest of 1 lemon

● **1** Preheat the oven to 200°C/400°F/Gas 6. Cook the pasta in a pan of boiling water according to the pack instructions until tender. Drain. Meanwhile, fry the bacon in a frying pan for 5 minutes until crisp. Set aside.

● **2** Mix together the pasta, bacon, tomatoes and four-cheese sauce. Pour into an ovenproof dish, sprinkle over the breadcrumbs and cheese and bake for 20 minutes until golden. Sprinkle with parsley and lemon zest to serve.

Calories per portion 820 Kcal ● Fat per portion 47g ● Serves 4

Serve with...
Serve the pasta bake with a green salad.

Why not try...
To freeze, assemble the dish but don't bake it. Cover and freeze. Thaw in the fridge overnight. Reheat at 180°C/350°F/Gas 4 for 35–40 minutes.

√√ *Extra Easy*   ✎ *Spicy*   Ⓝ *Contains Nuts*   Ⓥ *Vegetarian*

Roasted Red Pepper Pizza

Preparation time 5 minutes ● Cooking time 8 minutes

2 Italian basil pesto breads

150g pack Boursin (garlic and herb
   soft cheese)

10–12 peppadews (sweet piquante
   peppers sold in jars), roughly
   chopped

2 x 185g jars chargrilled red peppers,
   drained

6 cherry tomatoes

Salt and freshly ground black pepper

2 tablespoons chilli oil

Fresh basil leaves, to garnish

● **1** Preheat the oven to 200°C/400°F/Gas 6. Spread the Boursin over the breads, scatter with peppadews and arrange the chargrilled peppers on top. Add the cherry tomatoes and season with salt and black pepper.

● **2** Place on baking sheets and bake for 6–8 minutes until heated through. To serve, drizzle with chilli oil, cut in half and garnish with basil leaves.

Calories per portion 390 Kcal ● Fat per portion 13g ● Serves 4

Serve with...

Serve with a green salad and cooling yogurt and mint dip to drizzle on top.

Why not try...

If you can't find pesto breads, use garlic and coriander or plain naan breads instead. Allow 1 per person.

● *Make it at the Weekend* ✳ *Freeze it* Ⓥ *Vegetarian*

Mediterranean Lasagne

Preparation time 20 minutes ● Cooking time 1¼ hours

2 red onions, peeled

1 small aubergine, cut into chunks

2 courgettes, cut into chunks

2 red peppers, deseeded and cut into wedges

2 garlic cloves

Salt and freshly ground pepper

2 tablespoons olive oil

2 x 400g cans cherry tomatoes

2 tablespoons chopped fresh basil

2 tablespoons black olives, pitted and halved

2 tablespoons capers

6–8 sheets lasagne

for the sauce

2 eggs, beaten

2 x 250g tubs ricotta

150ml tub Greek yogurt

125g (4oz) mozzarella, grated

50g (2oz) Parmesan, grated

● **1** Preheat the oven to 220°C/425°F/Gas 7. Place the onions, aubergine, courgettes, peppers and garlic cloves in a baking tin, season with black pepper and pour over the oil. Toss together and roast for 25 minutes, stirring halfway through. Stir in the tomatoes and bake for 10 minutes.

● **2** Remove from the oven and reduce the heat to 180°C/350°F/Gas 4. Sprinkle the basil, olives and capers over the vegetables. In a bowl, mix together the eggs, ricotta and yogurt. Season well with salt and pepper.

● **3** Place half the vegetables in the base of an ovenproof dish and top with a third of the ricotta sauce, a third of the mozzarella and a layer of lasagne.

● **4** Repeat, starting with the remaining vegetables, then a third of the sauce, a third of the mozzarella and the remaining lasagne. Top with the remaining sauce, mozzarella and Parmesan. Bake for 30–40 minutes until golden.

Calories per portion 439 Kcal ● Fat per portion 26g ● Serves 6

Serve with...

Serve this tasty bake with a green salad.

 *Easy* ✔ *Spicy*

Pepperoni & Pepper Penne

Preparation time 10 minutes ● Cooking time 30 minutes

300g (11oz) penne

Salt and freshly ground black pepper

1 tablespoon oil

1 onion, chopped

3 garlic cloves, chopped

200g (7oz) pepperoni, sliced

1 red pepper, deseeded and sliced

125g (4oz) button mushrooms,

   halved

Pinch cayenne pepper

1 teaspoon sugar

Splash of red wine

500g carton passata

1 Cook the penne in a pan of boiling salted water according to the pack instructions until tender. Meanwhile, heat the oil in a frying pan and fry the onion and garlic until soft. Add the pepperoni, red pepper and mushrooms and fry for 2–3 minutes until slightly softened.

2 Stir in the cayenne pepper and sugar, then add the wine and passata, bring to the boil, reduce the heat and simmer for 20 minutes. Season with salt and freshly ground pepper. Drain the pasta and toss with the sauce.

Calories per portion 562 Kcal ● Fat per portion 21.6g ● Serves 4

Serve with...

**Top the pasta with freshly grated
Parmesan and serve with crusty bread.**

Why not try...

**if you are serving children, replace the
pepperoni with thin pork sausages.**

● *Quick* ✓✓ *Extra Easy*

Pasta with Broad Beans & Ham

Preparation time 5 minutes ● Cooking time 15 minutes

400g (14oz) short pasta, eg

   conchiglie, penne or fusilli

Salt and freshly ground black pepper

500g (18oz) frozen broad beans

1 tablespoon olive oil

1 red pepper, deseeded and roughly

   chopped

100g (3½oz) wafer-thin smoked

   ham, roughly chopped

150ml (¼pt) hot vegetable stock

2 tablespoons roughly shredded fresh

   basil

● **1** Cook the pasta in a pan of boiling salted water according to the pack instructions until tender. Add the broad beans for the last 3–4 minutes.

● **2** Heat the oil in a frying pan and cook the red pepper for 5 minutes. Add the ham and stock, and cook for a further 2 minutes.

● **3** Drain the pasta and beans and return to the pan. Stir in the peppers, ham and stock. Add the basil and season with salt and black pepper. Serve.

Calories per portion 490 Kcal ● Fat per portion 7g ● Serves 4

Serve with...

**Serve the pasta on its own or with
a mixed leaf salad.**

Why not try...

**You could replace the ham with cooked
chicken or turkey instead. Diced
mozzarella can also be added.**

Spanish-style Baked Pasta

Preparation time 10 minutes ● Cooking time 40 minutes

1 onion, chopped

2 tablespoons olive oil

1 green and 1 red pepper, deseeded
   and chopped

2 garlic cloves, roughly chopped

1 tablespoon sweet paprika

500ml (18fl oz) vegetable stock

500ml (18fl oz) passata

2 tablespoons pitted black olives

350g (12oz) spaghetti, broken into
   small pieces

Small handful chopped fresh parsley

● **1** Preheat the oven to 200°C/400°F/Gas 6. Heat the oil in a pan and fry the onion for 5 minutes until softened. Add the peppers and garlic and cook for 10 minutes over a low heat until softened. Stir in the paprika and cook for 30 seconds. Add the stock and passata. Bring to the boil. Add the olives.

● **2** Transfer the sauce to an ovenproof dish. Top with the spaghetti pieces and press down lightly so they are just covered by the liquid. Cover with a lid or foil and bake for 20 minutes until the pasta is just cooked. Sprinkle over the parsley and serve.

Calories per portion 420 Kcal ● Fat per portion 9g ● Serves 4

Serve with...

If you have a spare lemon, squeeze it over the pasta bake just before serving with salad and crusty bread.

Why not try...

For a meaty version add some chopped chorizo, or add prawns for a fish dish.

Weights, measures & temperatures

TEMPERATURE

°C	°F	Gas	°C	°F	Gas
110	225	¼	190	375	5
120/130	250	½	200	400	6
140	275	1	220	425	7
150	300	2	230	450	8
160/170	325	3	240	475	9
180	350	4			

MEASURES

Metric	Imperial	Metric	Imperial
5mm	¼in	10cm	4in
1cm	½in	15cm	6in
2cm	¾in	18cm	7in
2.5cm	1in	20.5cm	8in
3cm	1¼in	23cm	9in
4cm	1½in	25.5cm	10in
5cm	2in	28cm	11in
7.5cm	3in	30.5cm	12in

LIQUIDS

Metric	Imperial	Metric	Imperial
5ml	1 tsp	200ml	7fl oz
15ml	1 tbsp	250ml	9fl oz
25ml	1fl oz	300ml	½ pint
50ml	2fl oz	500ml	18fl oz
100ml	3½fl oz	600ml	1 pint
125ml	4fl oz	900ml	1½ pints
150ml	5fl oz/¼ pint	1 litre	1¾ pints
175ml	6fl oz		

WEIGHTS

Metric	Imperial	Metric	Imperial
15g	½oz	275g	10oz
25g	1oz	300g	11oz
40g	1½oz	350g	12oz
50g	2oz	375g	13oz
75g	3oz	400g	14oz
100g	3½oz	425g	15oz
125g	4oz	450g	1lb
150g	5oz	550g	1¼lb
175g	6oz	700g	1½lb
200g	7oz	900g	2lb
225g	8oz	1.1kg	2½lb
250g	9oz		

ABOUT THE RECIPES

Recipes that are suitable for freezing are indicated at the top of the recipe. For further guidance, see below and consult your freezer manufacturer's guidelines.

Food safety & hygiene

- Always wash your hands before handling any food.

- Always wash fruit and vegetables before using them.

- Ensure your work surfaces and chopping boards are clean. Keep a separate chopping board for preparing raw meat.

- Cool leftover food as quickly as possible, ideally within one to two hours, and then store covered in the fridge.

- Leftover rice must be stored covered and for no longer than one day.

- Do not buy cracked eggs.

- If you are reheating food, make sure you heat all the way through and until it is piping hot. Do not reheat food more than once. Do not keep leftovers for longer than two days.

- Once thawed, do not refreeze raw food unless you have cooked it first.

- Read and follow the use-by dates on packaging and jars.

- Children, pregnant women or the elderly should not eat recipes that contain raw eggs.

- Ensure that your fridge is 5°C or less and the deep freeze is at least -20°C.

- Change and wash tea towels, towels, dishcloths, aprons and oven gloves often. Keep your pets away from surfaces and tables.

- Organise your fridge so that meat is kept separately and on the bottom shelf. Keep dairy produce together and fruit, vegetables and salad ingredients in the salad compartment.

- Store raw foods separately from cooked foods to avoid contamination.

- After shopping, put all food for the refrigerator and freezer into their allotted places as soon as possible.